DrunkYard Dog

Tales

from Both Sides

of the Bar

Peter Carlaftes

THREE ROOMS PRESS

NEW YORK CITY

Interior Illustrations:
David Miller

Interior Photos:
Wendy Fitz

Cover and Interior Design:
Kat Georges Design, New York, NY
katgeorges.com

First Edition

Printed in the United States of America

ISBN: 978-0-9840700-4-6

Printed in the United States of America.
Text set in ITC New Baskerville.

Published by
Three Rooms Press, New York, NY
threeroomspress.com

to: *what's left* ....

from: *what isn't* ....

CONTENTS

SHEER BARDOM

For Scott.

*you'll never know
neither will I*

THE EXQUISITE TASTE OF CLEAR BILE

quarter of four
twenty below

one bartender
with
brain light
blinking
Lock The Door
Lock The Door
when
of course
said door
burst open
wielding
a brazen behemoth
sporting
a dark blue
snow-dusted
peacoat
who
was promptly
employed
a curt
Closed here, Pal

he corkscrewed up
wrapping claws
around the rail

I leaned over and sighed
Give it up my good man . . .

he broke the rail
lifting it skyward
like a paralytic
Thor
while using
his other paw
to swipe off
the snotsickles
frozen to his face

I warned the swaying mass
I have a gun behind the bar
trailing the rhetorical
Should I shoot you now?
then my tongue lashed
You may find this hard to believe, Buddy
but the proud owner of this shithouse
is times ten the asshole you are
and now I've gotta tell him
how his precious little bar-rail
was cracked off
by Mighty Joe Dung

Pea Coat passed me the pole
and lowering his head in lament
dislodged a phonic burp

I snapped
Here it is, Pal
You pay
Then you drink
Then you get the fuck out

he slipped off his coat
covered a barstool
and grunted
Dewars on the rocks

closing my eyes
I saw the owner
filling the Dewars
the day before
with cut-rate booze

sadly
I served Pea Coat

he sucked up the drink
ice and all

his eyes jumped
jack-box-weasel

then he puked clear bile
across the bar

as he rolled away
rerigging his coat
he turned
and said
Buddy . . .
That wasn't Dewars

ROTATE THE FISH

I was only working weekends
so my wife's *I'm Pregnant*
was the perfect time
to show responsibility

I called on this guy
by the name of Nil Feest
who wound up giving me
two nights starting
the following Tuesday

I achieved my goal with such swiftness
that my wife now felt we had a future

other than that
I tended bar in a clip-joint

my partner was Bernie
a stand-up
all around
fine-cut gem
who hated the boss
as much as I did

regardless of weather
or who was president
I'd always find Bernie
leaning on the backbar
chewing a cheap cigar
and following
the race results
over the phone

Friday after the sixth race
I told him about my new job

Bernie spit out his cigar
and reared back cursing
You're working for Nil Feest?
Fuck That Miserable Cocksucker!
He screwed over my two pals
Manny Gordon and Jimmy DeLido

he dialed the phone
and lit a new cigar
advising me softly
Keep an eye on him, Kid

watching Bernie tear up the losers
aroused my iron code of honor

Bernie was a sweetheart
and whatever he said
went
a page of concrete
in my book
so if he said
Nil Feest was a cocksucker
then, by god
Nil Feest was

it was time to walk tall
and do right by a friend

I called it
to myself
right there
that if Nil Feest uttered
one half-word wrong
I'd be out the door
before the little prick
took his next breath

the following Tuesday
I stood behind an empty bar
wearing a bright green apron

the place was of cajun motif
whatever the hell that meant

when the night manager
handed me the bank
with trembling voice
Mr. Feest will be in soon
I primed myself for combat

after two coffees and three cokes
me and twenty stools saw action

a fair-to-mid-life couple
on a business tryst
plunged in and started loin-pawing

for our happy hour presentation
the chef brought out plates of fish
deep-fried and blackened to stimulate thirst

I put a plate before the happy couple
but their hands remained occupied

indifferently
I set down
the other plates
in front of empty stools
thinking
what the fuck
let's have a seven-up
when
in walked the boss
right at me
head twitching

Nil Feest combined three words

Rotate the fish

fuck Audie Murphy
and fucking John Wayne
and motherfucking Gunga Din

I was out the door
apron off
in three tall steps

I strolled into the first bar
flashing a v-sign

on the homefront
my act of valiance received
an antonym of enthusiasm

I hid in the kitchen for three days
most likely reading Céline

Friday night
after the sixth race
I relived
each pivotal moment
with Bernie

he pulled at his cigar
laughing
Rotate the fish . . .
Ha Ha
He really said that?
Ha Ha
Nice work, Kid
Wait . . . Here's the seventh

Bernie didn't win the seventh

other than that
there is no
Was it worth it?

OVER (WITH A TWIST)

the night was
near the wire
when ill wind
swept through
the empty bar
blowing me
an ass-drunk
off-duty cop
waving a ten
and demanding
a beer
adding
the buddies-for-life
icebreaker
Cold . . . if you got

I gave him
a listless
I got
omitting
that what I got
was retina damage
from seeing his face

I did a quick shot

tilting his bottle
he toasted
Beer's sure cold, Buddy

I nodded with
shot number two

then this statue of pride said
Pal,
One crime should result
in a mandatory death penalty
and that's the crime of rape

I became a steamroller
and this bum was a bulge in the asphalt

I'd've shaved my body for an Oom-Pah Band

Okay, Pal
I theorized
Let's say
a police officer wakes up
one fine spring morning
wanting to screw his wife
but she's not in the mood
so later on he busts a kid
who deserves another chance
but because this cop's
holding his hard-on
they put the kid behind bars
where he takes it up the ass
and when the kid gets out
he commits a rape

Now can you really sit here and tell me
that you'd put this kid to death
just because some cop
couldn't fuck his wife
one fine spring morning?

hate on-duty flared up
but only sputtered out
That's why we got
guys like you in this world . . .
To think of things to say like that!

when I heard the bar door slam
I pocketed the change he left on the bar
and got about
as far as you can in this world
on seven bucks

BLACK CARPET TREATMENT

I often spend livelong days
musing those nights in bars

hell . . .
I spent
half my life
once
bartending
joints
owned by
skintight
pricks . . .
my
choice
specimens
being Rico
and the claptrap
he operated
five flights below
cheap to no end
called
The Showcase

even bums on the street shook their heads
each day I opened the doors for business

the only thing that tempered
the long hours of toil
was Rico's voice

his crackling harmonics
scraped the ear

in high-pitch overdrawl
like W.C. Fields
burdened by a chronic backache

I started working on
my Rico impression
at home

the seeds of my fancy
truly came to blossom
the night Rico emceed the show
to a congregation of born yesterdays

I never could fathom
what possessed anyone
to set foot in The Showcase
but this night was beyond priceless

the pre-show air tittered electric
the spotlight hit centerstage

Rico rolled up his eyes
and stuck out his chest

when he pushed in his butt
the room howled asking for more
so Rico built them a dream . . .

Do you know whose career began on this stage?

the hush spread awe among the spellbound

proudly
he revealed
Andrea DeLorin sang her first song on this very stage

DeLorin was only a budding hopeful
yet each eye kindled such reverence
you would've thought
the headliner was Jesus

I became so totally preoccupied
perfecting my Rico impression
that people thought I was nuts

my shining moment came when
Rico let me emcee the show

I gave that crowd
a Rico impression
to die for . . .

Do you know whose career began on this stage?
Klaus Barbie killed his first audience on this very stage

the only chuckle
came from a comic backstage
so I gave him a rousing intro
and returned to duty
behind the bar
then
quickly
fell out of love
with the hard buck
and as my days
bartending
The Showcase
dwindled down
I lucked onto a job
in a real night club
where most of the guys knew Rico

the whole crew
loved my Rico
at first
but love is ephemeral . . .

so I put the bit to rest
until
one day
a payphone
painted me a picture

I called The Showcase

Rico answered
This is Rico

I said
This is Rico

he asked
Who is this?

I said
It's Rico

he said
I'm Rico

I said
I'm Rico

he said
Hold on

I heard him
inform the cook
I bought steaks on sale
but they smell bad so . . .
Serv'em with pepper sauce

when he
came back
asking
Who is this?
I was flush

my Rico now had a new life

the guys went
ga-ga
later that night

two captains
four comics
and a waiter
positioned
themselves
anxiously around
the other extensions
while the phone rang

Rico answered

live shows were in progress
at both ends of the conversation

Rico said
This is Rico

I said
This is Rico

he asked
Who is this?

I said
It's Rico

he said
I'm Rico

I said
I'm Rico

he said
Hold on

man oh man
were we crying

the mad round
mounted
as a surprise guest star
(his wife Dorothy)
(no deep thinker)
took the phone and asked
Who is this?

I said
It's Rico

she said
No it's not

I said
It's Rico . . . Your husband

She said
Rico's here . . . Who is this?

the customers found us more entertaining
than the undercurrent of comedy on stage

once back
Rico asked
Is this Chucky?

I said
No . . . It's Rico

he said
I'm Rico

I said
I'm Rico

he said
Hold on

we were holding our sides
while people at The Showcase
underzealously applauded
some dazed comic coming offstage
to the raging Rico rally
We love you . . . They love you . . . Come back

then intimately
Rico cautioned his wife
See if that chicken's cooked on table twenty

anyone else
would've hung up
immediately
but Rico returned
and asked
Who is this?

pandemonium broke loose
busboys were on the floor
and nothing else mattered
except talking to Rico . . .

I'll always remember that golden night
he cascaded into The Showcase
followed by a funny little fat man
weighed down with paint supplies

they stacked up the tables and chairs
and painted the rug over pitch black
with old rollers

somewhere
in mid-stroke
Rico muttered
You can't believe what they want
for a carpet these days . . .

yeah . . .
those days
those nights

hell . . .
I spent
half my life
once

INHABITING THE MOMENT

I've been here drinking
at the end of this bar
for the past three hours

I prefer to sit
at the end of the bar
because
this strategic position
eliminates
the grim probability
of being stuck between two assholes

I lean back to drain the watery remains from my glass
and my eyes transfix upon the obedient round clock
hanging over the backbar

it's 5:30 [bar time]
meaning: it's ten after five [real time]
meaning: [real or not] time doesn't matter
meaning: I should ask [myself] what does

instead
I tell Scott
Gimme another

he scoops a glass into the ice
and grabs a bottle from the well
like it was his lungs at work or something

Scott holds my drink
and says
Pace yourself, Pal
The sun's still up

a young girl sits on the next stool

I propel a leer at Scott
while thinking
This girl's too young
What could I say to her?
I don't know where Madonna's on tour

Scott asks her
Whaddaya have?

she hems [haws]
and oohs [ahhs]
Hmmm . . .
I'm waiting for a friend

Scott walks off
unimpressed

Tequila [the song]
overpours from the jukebox

some just-off-work mechanics
from the brake shop
'round the corner
are whooping up a ruckus
at the other end of the bar

Scott barks
Keep it down, boys

the goliath of the group
hollers from the rail
We Need Shots Gold

I swallow half my drink and zone out
going back . . .
way back . . .
all the way back to last night [this morning]
when I closed the bar
and sat with some pals
having
cocaine-inflicted conversations

shots all around and another line
shots all around and another line

Hey! kick the juke—this record is stuck

Hah!
I don't believe it
but
Tequila [the song]'s
now stuck on the jukebox
in convergence with my own metaphor

big-body-brake-shop headbutts the jukebox

his people laugh slapping high-low high-fives
and I drift back to morning
climbing into bed and clicking the remote

now [then] playing on the late, late show
was the film version of Steinbeck's Cannery Row
and I was rocked to sleep by a pounding heart

today began prone
playing catch the remote
until boredom growled
so I put on clothes
because what I wanted
waited at the bar

the front door swings open
and the girl next to me
jumps up
screaming
Caitlin! Caitlin!
and I watch the two embrace . . .

their eyes seemingly lie fallow inside
interchangebly vacuous fields of vision

they order white wine
and, in one breath
the girl named Caitlin says
Kelly . . .
You won't believe what happened to
my Aunt Ethel and her friend Wanda
while they were on vacation in Waikiki
staying in one of those fancy hotels

After one last day on the beach
they went back to the hotel and
their room had been burglarized

The thief took everything
except Wanda's camera

They thought it was strange for a thief
to leave an expensive camera on the bed
but what could they do?

They came home last week and
Wanda had the film developed
so they'd see all the exciting places
Know what I mean?

the girl named Kelly
nods her head
listening intently
as was I

the girl named Caitlin continues

The final exposure was a close-up
of two objects
protruding from a man's butt

Those objects were their toothbrushes
Can you believe it?

That creep shoved their toothbrushes
up his butthole
and left them on the sink

What a sicko!
God knows how he took the picture

I spit out a laugh on the edge of inhaling some vodka

Their faces flash me perfect How Dare You's

Sorry, Girls, I say
with drunken nonchalance
but I couldn't help overhearing
the plight of your poor Aunt Ethel

There's something wrong with that guy
Hawaii 5-0 better put him away
I mean, not only is he a thief
but he made sure that your Aunt and her friend
found out they were sucking his shit for a week

the girl named Kelly shrieks
C'mon, Caitlin
Let's get a table

I snigger
What's this, Girls . . . Double Indignity?

I yell at Scott
Gimme a double, Pal
I can't taste the vodka

a guy enters with two pretty ladies
and they sit behind me at a table

the guy looks familiar
but I can't place him . . .
not for the cliched life of me

Wait . . . I got it !
in Cannery Row . . .
Jesus Mary Joseph
it's the guy who played
Jesus Mary Joseph

I lunge
hellbent

three sets of eyes turn

I ask
through a cupped hand
Are you Jesus Mary Joseph?

he says
Get the fuck away from me

he thinks I'm horning in
on the women

a new girl sits on the next stool

this one reminds me of the dark gals
in those colorful paintings by Gaugin
with the fruit hanging off their boobs

I slur out the perfect inquiry

Hey, Doll . . .
Do you know Gaugin?

she spins away to spew mindtrash
with a kid still cutting baby teeth

from behind
Scott whispers
Here comes the night

the jukebox howls
Here Comes The Night

drawing closer
Scott asks
What'll it be . . .

who knows . . .

maybe Scott and I
stayed there
drinking til the end
like we did
the week before . . .

or maybe
we found
some place
where
dreams extend
beyond last call

Illustration:
Them by Miller
(detail)

LOOSE JOINTS ONE

For
Henry Chinaski

GOOD COMPANY

sitting on a bar
you can discover
everything you need
to know about a woman
by looking at her hands

have another drink
and I'll tell you
some more bullshit

HOW DOES LOVE TASTE

I sat
on a barstool
tuning in and out
to the voice of a friend
extolling the virtues of his
new found love

she
was like an angel
and boy was she built

I told him
I'm happy for you, man
can't wait to meet her

a week later
he tells me
she sucked his cock

after swallowing his semen
she
licked her lips
then

lifting her head
she said
Fred
you really need to put
more kelp in your diet

he is now
a doctor of holography
in the midst
of marriage number four

he never met another woman
who could identify
the different levels
of vital elements in his semen

Through the labyrinth of
Regret
I see that faded youth

forsaking the future

like it was never gonna
happen

REFUGE IN E MINOR

if you can find comfort
while shitting out your guts
on a toilet in some strange bar
then you have what it takes
to believe in yourself
and others like you

I DRINK, THEREFORE I GLOW

full bar

lots of faces

the clock is gone

I'm getting there

the guy to my right
gets serious

I tell him
Man
If for whatever reason
you had ten grand in your pocket right now
and needed somebody to hold it for you
I'd be there

I may not be there tomorrow
But at least you believed in the moment

somebody slaps my back

Damn, it's Joe

pointing to my right
I say
Joe
You ever meet my friend, Bob?

THE BAR ESSENTIALS

For Later
(when Goodtime Charlie knows)

DO ME NEXT

Taxi!

son of a bitch bastard
with an off-duty light

Hey, Jeff
Stand up

You look like you need an ambulance
not a taxi

for the fifteenth time
he slurs out
The Cloisters
The Hellfire Club
or
The Staten Island Ferry
one of the three
over and over
always
whenever we close the bars
and wind up walking the streets
wondering why
the daylight was ever invented

Jeff
just came off
love gone wrong
spending numb
six months on the sofa
while a woman wailed
Why don't you move
I can't love you anymore

he finally found himself a small studio
in a welfare building on the Upper West Side
across the street from a discount liquor store
with dead-eyed clerks behind bulletproof glass

staring out his window
at poor faces
sitting on stoops

passing hollow days
pouring hot water
directly into
Cup O' Soup packs

chasing broth
with cheap red wine

I'm always there for Jeff
anytime he feels
like facing the outside world

hit some bars
meet some girls

Hey, Jeff . . .
This is Diane

behind eyes long gone
he releases
the perceptibly
unclever remark
Frankie . . .
Meet Johnny

Unimpressed
Diane turns to me and says
Your friend is very bitter

we're on the street now
sun's getting brighter
and he's ranting on
about The Hellfire Club
a warehouse of perversion
near the river on 14th

a taxi stops

Thank you Jeff, for standing up
We're going to The Hellfire Club

neither of us had ever been

10 bucks to get in
5 for a watered down drink
800 men surrounding
one fat blonde
and a thin girl
standing by the bar

Jeff wanders off
so I approach the girl
and announce
I'm a heterosexual

she lifts up her dress
and yanks on her penis

Jeff's sitting at a table

I tell him
Let's get out of here

he wants to stay

the crowd is writhing
to a dance-beat frenzy

some guy tries to kiss me
and somebody else
is working my belt off

I spin around
and squirm my way
to the front door

someone stamps my hand
so I can get back in

Taxi!

I tell the little brown man
behind the wheel
7th Avenue
Downtown

he asks me with a smile
Where is this 7th Avenue?

I look at his ID card
hanging on the glovebox

his first name
is five consecutive vowels

inside this same moment
Jeff was watching the fat blonde
go down on a line of men
one after the other
come one, come all

Jeff sidled up

Tenderly
he pleaded to her
Do Me Next

she removed the cock from her mouth
and without hesitation
screamed
Get Out!

two bouncers carried him to the street
he didn't have a dime in his pockets

this is the nadir
of any man's life

completely broken
he married the first girl
to say yes

later
his wife
gave birth to triplets

I had a vision of Jeff
the moment my wife
told me she wanted out

closing my eyes
I saw Jeff sprout wings
as if he'd heard
his own wife
say the same words

in the dark
I could see Jeff
flying up
way off above
over
every piece of madness
but when I opened my eyes
it was my wife sitting there
and she's long gone now

being alive is about these moments

if there were an answer
then even these moments
would be long gone now

HAND TO MOUTH

forget about sleep

Jim and I were on
a sixteen-hour drunk

even the thought of
waking up
sounded too painful
to us
so
at six in the morning
we stumbled to the Irish bar
a block and a half from
his place

and once we were settled
with drinks in our hands
I was certain
no God created
any of the faces
illuminated by
glints of sunlight
shining through
rising smoke
from the ashtrays

nobody went to the toilet

this
was sawdust-sprinkled
No-Exit stenchialism
more necessary
than any other
make-believe moment

Charlie was working
the stick that morning
dragging around
a dark grimace
that intensified
each time he walked past
this sunken-faced drunk
chewing on a cigar butt
down the other end of the bar

How 'bout a drink
inquired the drunk

Give it a rest, Bert
Charlie replied
as he poured Bert a shot of well whiskey

Thanks a lot Charlie
said Bert
You broken-off prick of a man

Charlie went off
to sulk

I asked Jim why Charlie
didn't throw this bum out

Jim told me, *He can't*
Bert's his albatross
you see
Charlie and Bert come from
different counties
but after the war
they came over from Ireland
on the same boat

Now Charlie had a job waiting
but Bert had to scratch around
and some nights he got pretty hungry
so
hoping to lick out the pots
or something
he'd climb the stairs
and knock on the door
of Charlie's cold-water flat

Charlie would open the door
but the cupboard was always bare

Now Charlie comes from
what is known as
the cheapest county in
Ireland

one evening
Charlie went down the hall to the john
while Bert searched the floor for crumbs

Bert took a peek in the icebox
nothing inside but a swallow of milk

Bert slid open
the top dresser drawer

inside
sat a plate
of warm corned beef
accompanied by
potatoes and cabbage

when Charlie got back
Bert began yelling
Ya miserable prick
I'm starving out there
and you're in here
hoarding your dinner
in the top drawer

it's been forty years
and Bert still shows up
every morning that Charlie
works a shift

Charlie returned to his post

Bert stood up
and said
See ya, Charlie

and Charlie said
See ya now, Bert

there's much to be admired inside
the temperament of the Irish soul

Charlie wiped the bar down

two old reeling bald guys
sat down and ordered drinks

turning their heads
in opposite directions
one snarled
Cunt
and the other shrieked
Love

Charlie shook his head
sadly to the heavens

I looked at Jim in expectation

Oh . . .
he said smiling
glad to tell a story
That's Tom and Bob
The Battling Brothers
they've been coming here for years . . .

SOME ARE OYSTERS

Goodtime Charlie! How you Doing?

Breaking Even, answered Charlie
then took the next stool and ordered
VO and Plain Water . . .

we'd both just got off work
tending bar at other joints

see
Charlie worked on Bleecker Street
but lived on Staten Island
so there were nights he'd make the ferry
and take the bus from that side home
though when he had a real good night
he caught a cab for 30 bucks

Goodtime Charlie always proffered
Some Days are Oysters,
Some are Pearls . . .

see
now—last week
when Charlie
took a cab
he fell asleep
and when the driver
woke him up
the meter said
46 bucks
so Goodtime Charlie
went ballistic
shouting

Look, You Slimy Bastard!
The Fare is 30 Bucks!
but the cabbie only pointed
You Mister—Look the Meter!
so Charlie told him
I don't pay you Dollar One!
then went inside and slammed the door
while cabbie threatened, *I Call Cops!*

Charlie brushed his teeth
and climbed into bed
but
soon came a banging at his door
so he opened it to Cop
standing next to Cabbie yelling
Yes! He the One!
That the Man!
He owe 40 and 6 dollars!

Well
Goodtime Charlie reared back
and informed the cop
The meter's always 30 bucks
He tried to pull a fast one
which
turned the tide
in Charlie's favor
for the moment
until the cop asked to see
his ID for his report
but
when Charlie pulled his wallet out
along came a little
glassine packet of coke

and the cop turned his back
roaring
Look Pal, Pay up—Now!
to which
Charlie promptly did
and
after picking up the packet
disappeared behind the door

Yeah, muttered Charlie
Some are Oysters
Some are Pearls . . .

THE MAN WITH NO PLAN

Two wrong cats
came in the bar
looking to upset
the order of things
so quickly, the bartender
picked up the phone
and called
the police department

the duo of dim
saw their scheme
fizzle out
so they split the scene
before
the squad car
pulled up

well
I knew a few guys
in the district
so I stumbled outside
and beamed —*Hey!
Is Ronnie Here?
How 'bout the Paws?*

the cop shot a glance
at my wrists
then his handcuffs
so I hightailed it back
to my seat in the bar

while a few of the guys
more sober than I
explained to the cop
what went down

now
right about then
my friend Ronnie pulled up
and the first thing he said
to his cohort was
Do you know if Petey is here?

somebody told me
that Ronnie was there

I ran out the door
and gave him a hug

we sat on his car
and shot bit of breeze
while
the other cop
stood by
reluctantly erect
until
jumping in his car
and peeling off

Ronnie came back
after his shift broke
and bought me a drink
at the bar
then the bartender
got us the next round . . .

I never laid eyes
on that
other cop again
and there are nights
I remember that
in my prayers

ODE TO UNCLE WILLIE

he sat on a barstool and ordered a drink
I poured the drink and set it before him
treating the moment as if it were
the most important time in both our lives

that is how
I believe
a good bartender
should operate

later he became Willie
cocaine dealer
ex-jarhead
shot up in 'Nam
the battle of Hue
a man without a country
burning bridges
with reckless abandon

recently I'd moved
from New York
to San Francisco
and often missed
the all night hang
so several times
Willie and I
saw the sunrise
through a bar window

when Willie wasn't in the bar
people said things like:
Poor guy was in Vietnam
and
He can't get his life together
and
His cocaine is cut to shit

one day I worked the morning shift
and the chef cooked me ham and eggs

I left the steaming plate on the bar
while I restocked the liquor bottles

there was a loud knock
on the front door
and I turned my head

Willie was there
looking like Atlas
after dropping the whole damn world

I went around the bar
and let him in

Willie!
What the hell you doing up so early?

Now Willie's voice sounded like
somebody talking in their sleep
after swallowing a handful of lime

I can't get to bed, he said
I'm in a room with Lucy on Lombard

he saw my breakfast on the bar
and asked
Whose is that?

I told him to sit down and eat
the chef would make me another

Willie sat on a stool and began
shoveling food in his mouth

I moved some bottles
to the backbar
and in the mirror
watched Willie's nose
drip blood on
the eggs
and he just kept eating

I didn't say a word

now the law of averages dealt Willie
some serious trouble in San Francisco

I told Willie
Move to New York

Nobody has anything for you here
except misplaced pity

In New York
Everybody is as fucked up as you

I guess in the long run
he didn't have a choice

he caught the red-eye
to New York
with no baggage

Manhattan and Willie
embraced one another

he sold his wares
and drank in bars
till the sun came up
earning
the nickname
Uncle Willie

the last thing I heard about Willie
he was sitting on a bar in the Village

Hey Uncle Willie
gimme a quarter
Thanks, Uncle Willie
catch you tomorrow

an old lady in a wheelchair
with a shawl in her lap
appeared on the street
outside the bar

she couldn't seem to talk
or move herself about
and she was
pointing desperately
at something

a bunch of drunks were looking around
What's she pointing at?
Is she in trouble?

Willie came out of the bar
and immediately put great importance
into where she was pointing

he told the crowd
She's pointing across the street
She wants to go across the street

he bent over her
and said
You want to go across the street
I'll push you across the street

he pushed her across the street
and gently lifted her chair
onto the sidewalk

he moved around
the wheelchair
and faced the woman
assuring her
You're okay now
You're across the street

the old lady pulled out a stun gun
from underneath her shawl
and shot Willie high in the chest

Willie passed out cold on the concrete

Some regulars carried him back in the bar
and stuck him in the corner
by the pinball machine

Later Willie came around
stumbled to the bar
and ordered a drink

his money was no good

everyone was buying

Yo, Uncle Willie
I guess that old douchebag
didn't want to cross the street

How many times
you been shot
Uncle Willie?

A toast to Uncle Willie

glasses clinking

Hey, Uncle Willie
gimme a quarter
Thanks, Uncle Willie
catch you tomorrow

The Last Cocktail Waitress (on Earth) I will ever come on to

For
I do believe
her name was
Julie

Illustration:
Overbite by Miller

once came time
to
draw the line
_____

swearing off
coming on
to any
cocktail waitress

no matter how
they held a bottle
or pushed their breasts
against the bar
after
hearing
enough patter
I was through . . .

the town was
Tucson, Arizona
at this jazz bar
where
they'd
pour me triples
every
other
on the house
so—there I'd sit
most every night
in a Seven
7th Heaven
getting sloshed
until a Friday
early spring

when a visioness
appeared

this
trim
blonde, blue-eyed ballad
with a bedroom-begging
build

lust/love
didn't matter
I just fell

getting
steamed up
in the men's room stall
her groping, us smooching
me—prodding (for more)

while tonguing her ear
me cooing Tonight
so gentle —her answer
Can't
Gotta Work a Double
or (the next time)
Can't Tomorrow
Got Astrology Class
then I'd sulk back
to the bar
with bulge
in pant

but the third time
(the last time)
she pushed me
too far
with some yarn
about her landlord
and
deposit overdue

sure

so I drove home
determined
to deform our future

and
before I hit
the pillow

(pow!)

the muse came
unto thee

so excited
couldn't sleep

jump start
till next night

fifteen minutes before closing
I smeared dirt on my face
and stormed into the bar

Doll
I Gotta Flat
and My Fuckin' Jack Broke
So—if it's not a Problem
Would you mind if I use Yours?

She bit
I had her keys
which I used
to pop her trunk
and leave ajar
'cause I didn't have a flat
I had a plan

I brought her back the keys
then hopped into her trunk
and held the latch down
so it wouldn't either
pop up or shut

then
immediately
of course
I had to pee
(motherfuck)

when only
15 minutes later
she jumped in
and turned the key

but
as
her foot
let out the clutch
some dirtclod
tapped the window
charming
Wanna Smoke a Joint?
fucker!
(6 x motherfuck)
need I say
she let him in

they started to toke
and
giggle/giggle
as I listened
to the lamest
talk on earth

*Were the Doobie
Brothers better
before Michael
MacDonald?*

My God
I wanted
to jump out
and pee
with one hand
and kick his ass
with the other
but I wasn't
giving up

so I held
as she gave him the slip
with one where
she visits dad's grave
and even though
I felt sorry
for the poor dork
I was feeling
much worse
for myself
when
she pulled up
some driveway
then stopped

(pop!)

out I came
dick in hand

she screamed
What the hell you Doing?

I said—*Peeing*
which I'd started
ala river
down the drive

I'll be right
with you, Doll

she claimed
My Boyfriend's Home Inside

(poof!)

the curtains
in the window
through the carport
moved on cue

And he owns
a Gun Collection

mission over
time to shoo

I zipped up
and told her
No matter what
I made it home
with you

then turned
and hit the dark

henceforth
to never put it
out there
for a dolly with
a tray

as I headed
towards a place
between
myself
and distant mountain
lost within
my thoughts
this voice from nowhere
asked *You Pete?*

so I looked up
at nothing there
but to my right
sat some guy
in a cab
who asked again
You Pete?

I nodded, *Yeah*

He said
Some Girl
called you a Cab

I said *OK*
and jumped on in
then told him
what had just
gone down

he laughed
Hey, Pete
The taxi ride's
on me

NIGHT CLUB CONFIDENTIAL

For
Susan
and the night

HALF A HEAD

pre-tense
in tow
a night
once
yonder
I worked
on water
pouring
liquid
mirage

a good dive
where the boss
let me be . . .

current
spread
cream of
blonde
over heel

told me
she was
an artist . . . .

tuesday
welded
nineteen
forever

couldn't
keep her eyes
off me . . .

the last
pair a dice
lost
tap doubt
locals
left
abroad
demanned

sorrow galore
has got to go
but I'll break it
very gently . . .

Aaahharrgghhemm
Closed, Hon

when I reach
for her glass
she makes off
with my hand . . .

outcast
palm
swept
flat side
clear
atop
point coif
when
What!
where
should've
been
skull
wasn't

the girl had only
half a head . . .

Oh—God—Wow!
Lady—Jesus,
What Happened?

seems
these two men
in a van
grabbed her
right off
the street
then
raped her
in turn
and
tossed her . . .

What Did The Cops Do?

seems
they
tried to
rape her
too . . .

I couldn't
be the next guy

Get Out!

strip
mindshaft
long
dark sense
her distant
staccato

past
clutter
without
choice
redeems
time
being
for what
time
being
with choice
would
comprise
at best
such a
bittersweet
once

I hear
home
now
in a heel
click
echo
where nights
were just me
and the water

SURROUNDED BY OTHERS

here comes Alice

short blonde gal

her face
a circuit
of never enough . . .

she orders
Tanqueray and tonic

I pour well gin

she looks the other way . . .

Alice doesn't
want
to be forty

in the dark
she's a nurse . . .

Alice has
a brother, Freddie

good
jazz pianist

had a gig here
not long back

but
the poor cat melted
after just one set . . .

bent
over
the bar
he broke
Look, Man
I'm losing my mind

There's this Greek girl
who lives above me and
she's fixed it so I can't go home

startled
I asked
How'd she do that?

Well
he leaned in
They started drilling
upstairs through her wall
last week
and long black limos
are parking on the street
by the building next door
so it must be a plant
where the mob
makes drugs
and they're keeping all their stuff
in the Greek girl's apartment
but, she knows that I know
so the guinneas got to kill me

The only thing that got him
was Bellevue
two weeks later . . .

Alice spent visits
watching nurses
in the hall
until a paper
told Freddie
his mind mended . . .

he's been in
twice
since he got
sprung

told me both times
they stopped drilling

Uh Oh
here he comes now . . .

a regular asks me
What's wrong?

I roar back
You're what's wrong, Pal
You ain't tipped me all night!

I bring Freddie
a club soda

behind
wistful eyes
he responds
Remember the Greek girl
who lives up from me?

I nod slowly
watching Alice pose
for two new guys
playing
What'cha Doing Later . . .

chin
down
Freddie spills
Hey
Listen
I'm desperate, Man
Now she's up there
strutting around the floor
every fucking night
wearing black high heels

and even though
I never seen 'em
I just know
they're fucking black

and I sit there
and I listen
and I can't do nothing else

Alice yells
Ordering

I scoot over
to the well
eye-darting
her brother
sideways . . .

Alice whispers
What do you think?

I assure
He's fine

she calls out
Two Tanqueray and tonics

I pour well gin

she pleads
Use Tanqueray
I like these guys

ONE BAR TO THE NEXT

here goes
another
lock snap
Sunday
spreading
gate-rattle
Monday
short
3 block
stroll
pre-dawn
for
the
paper
then a cab
down
town
to the bar
that's
tended
by
god bless
my old pal
Jim

there's
a soot
glazed bum
all bone
skin gaunt
ankled
to his pants
up the street

now
a cheese
coated cock
never did strike
no sparks in me
hell
I've seen
these
saints
sleeping on
piss-soaked
benches
before
but
still I turn
and
a quite thin
foot long
ripe to fall
turd
curls down
from
his crack
and I feel blessed

does
a turd
make noise
when
no one
hears it fall?

up ahead
under
neon
is the newsstand
where
every week
a Korean
asks me
if I want
The Form
thanks
to when
I did buy
one
from him
about
a year ago
and
uncanny
how
this
shrewd
little bugger
can
still
remember
my purchase
after
all his
many
transactions
since

across
the street
a priest
waits
fresh
from
the newsstand
with
a magazine
rolled up
under
his arm

the light
changes

the priest
and I
traverse

the Korean
tears ass
from
his store
screaming
and jumps
the priest
in mid-street
jarring
loose Time
to reveal
the priest's
hidden plunder:
Hot Young Studs Who Want
Hard Black Dick

I grab
a paper
off the rack
and the Korean
comes in
behind me
counting
crumpled ones

he asks
You Want Racing Form?

the guy
doesn't
miss a trick

Okay, Pal

what the fuck
maybe
the bum can
wipe
his ass
with it

Yo, Cab

I tell the driver
Take Me Downtown

leaning back
I close my eyes

Ha
wanna bet
next time
the priest
comes in
the Korean asks
You Want Afro Buddy Buttfuck?

I roll
the window
halfway
down
and light
a cigaret

the driver yells
Put Out That Cigaret!
Put Out That Cigaret!
Put Out That Cigaret!

a big fat kid
who whines
like a whale
born with
too small
a blowhole

I toss my smoke
and tell him
Shut The Fuck Up

skidmarks
on 2nd Avenue

the kid yanks out
a crowbar
and huffs around
to my side
shouting
Get Outta That Cab!
Get Outta That Cab!
Get Outta That Cab!

I've
had
enough

rolling
the rest of
the window
away
I point
to my head
and snarl at him
Come On, You Fat Fuck
Do Me In Right Here
Hit Me, Motherfucker

calmly
the kid says
You Could Put Me In The
Hospital
With That Cigaret

squaring up
I tell him
Kid
You Belong In A Hospital

I flag down
the next cab
and the kid wails
Don't Pick Him Up!
Don't Pick Him Up!
Don't Pick Him Up!

the new driver
asks me
What The Fuck's That?

he's a thin old black
who looks like
he plays the horses

I slip him The Form
and he seems happy

leaning back
I close my eyes
and Jim says
Stoli
Soda
as the jukebox speaks
the first smooth strands
of Artie Shaw
serenading
These Foolish Things

HE FUCK YOU ANYWAY

Susan, Dear
We'd Like Two More

I've been stool right
to my pal, Shawn
talking fat people
for 3 drinks . . .

Thanks, Sue
You're The Best

uh—make that
4 drinks . . .

Now Shawn just had me crying
through this one about a fat man
with a huge schlong
at some nude beach
on Long Island
and
I need a good bit
to get back the laugh
so I'm searching the bar
(aren't we all)

now, the fat man
paraded up and down
this beach
day after day
with all other nudes
admiring his goods

until one day, struck
by a stray volleyball,
his cock just dropped
to the sand
strap and all

hot damn!
here comes
bonafide bar slut . . .

down the bar
Susan's busy
with her boyfriend
chewing glum . . .

Hey, Gals
I'm In Love

Sue looks at Shawn like
has he lost what little was left . . .

I push my hair back in the mirror
leering at this silly skank
that I'd rather see floating down the river
than fuck drunk at 5 a.m.
but I got Shawn hooked bad
so I'm going for broke . . .

Do You Have A Comb
In Your Purse, Shawn
Or A Brush
I Might Borrow?

the time's ripe . . .

I stand up and trip
on the first stool
and fall down
flat on my face . . .

two guys rush over
to help and as they
pull me off the floor
I stick my tongue out
razzing Shawn

Two more, Sue
And Get Sad Sack One
And Tell Him
Love Has Its
Ups And Downs

Hey—Almost Forgot
The Chinese Girl, Shawn
Lulu Introduced Us.
I Thought She Really Liked Me—
What Can I Say?
What's Not To Like?

Susan's
serving pints
to living shit
in yellow ties . . .

Usually Oriental Girls
Mistrust Me at First Sight
But this One Only Smiled
as we Both Spun
Through the Night . . .

It was Easy
and We Made It
Just a Monday . . .

Anyhow
I Ran into Lulu Yesterday
and Asked Her for the
Chinese Girl's Number
And Here's What Lulu Told Me
That the Chinese Girl Told Her

She Said
Pete, The Kind of Guy You Say
You No Wanna Fuck Him
He Fuck You Anyway

and now I'm one up

Shawn owes me big time

and believe me
it's good to be wrong

RAZORTHINEDGE

dawn spat
on the city
and I got tossed
from the bar

too late to go home
too early for work
so
I stretched out
on a bench
and
started to drift
when
the sudden
burst
of a siren
stunned me

a sadistic cop
in a squad car
smirked
Hey, Buddy
You Can't Sleep Here
then
tooled along
to roust awake
the next unlucky soul

an old black man
sat down and said
They're Trying To Kill Me

when I asked
Who?
he shuddered
Everyone

I decided to take care of him
being he looked so terrified
so I flashed him my razor
and said, *Don't Worry, Man*
Nobody's Gonna Mess With You

side by side
the sun brightened

I stood up and said,
C'mon, Pal
I'll Walk You Out Of The Park

his eyes
grew
his face
fell
and he said, *Man*
You got that razor

he'd be seeing my razor held
now in every stranger's hand

I didn't waste
no more time

I was busy
looking
for someone
who needed me

LOOSE JOINTS TWO

For
Al & The Suzy Q,
Ronnie & The Paws

Illustration:
Them by Miller
(detail)

IT LIVES

back
one glorious
prior 9/11 day
when flying first class
under someone else's name
and somehow still awake
after drinking 3 days
while looking
something more
like—what
the cat dragged in
(dragged in)
I gurgled—

    Pillow

at the girl and she complied behind a sneer
where I by clocked out until mid-flight
upon hearing the booze cart draw near
—my left eye
popped open
as right there
she stood to
playfully
reckon

    It lives!

then—out of her way
I started anew
with champagne glass-full
that would do

SERVICE (WITH A SMILE)

How the hell
did
me and Al
make it
back by 6 pm
to work a party
at the bar?

there was no answer

yet—there we stood
barely standing
on this
night of all nights
to
get stuck with
a new barback

there he was
—this
elderly
short/bald
Chinese man
with a mouthful of gold
all smile

me and Al
both squashed
smiled back

who gave fuck?

the fellow didn't know
vodka from ice

so we began his career
by filling
two glasses with vodka
and downing
the contents of both
to take the edge off
passing time
'till 7:30
when 200
handfull's
showed up—so
I stuck our little man
on a stool in the far corner
and we started
doing battle
with a bunch
worth next to nothing
and though the clock
seemed not to move
time—as always
still went by

we'd almost made it
so
I asked Al
What if you get
these bums out
and I get our friend
to help me clean up?

his answer
was more vodka

now on to task
at hand

I had our friend
stand 'side the well
and watch me
as I cleaned a glass
between the brushes
in the sink
below the bar—then
stepping back
pointed, *Your Turn*
and
now
my turn
to watch
as he
looked at the glass
then the sink
then the bar
and
then
the fruit tray
caught his eye

he grabbed the bin
full of fresh limes
dumped them in the trash
washed out the bin
then put the bin back

next—the olives
then—the cherries
Oh, Jeezus
I burst
screaming *Al!*
as I hit
the floor

Al ran back
to find me—gasping
Look!

so Al looked
as our friend
dumped a pint glass
of new straws
in the trash
whereby—which time
Al also hit the floor

rolling 'round bar mats
soaked smelly
with booze
while
a large stack
of unused napkins
was next batch to go

and
once again
me and Al
drank till dawn . . .

well
now
the boss
put our friend
in the kitchen
with our blessing
and we waited
for the day
he'd clean
the walk-in

SIR BREATHE

'twas new year's day
once dusk
leaning back
in a booth
still as stone
while even the food
turning cold on my plate
seemed amazed
I remained sitting up
when calmly,
with kindness,
the sweet owner's wife
bent over affirming

Sir, Breathe

and soon
after heeding
the lady's advice
I continued
to call it
a night

THE WORLD SMILES WITH YOU

I can't remember exactly
what happened that night
but apparently
what happened
was:

while driving home drunk
at three in the morning
I stopped my car
and fell asleep
smack in the middle of
The Golden Gate Bridge

Two cops swore under oath
that they pulled up behind me
banged on the window
and the first thing I said
was:

> *Your Honor*
> *I'm waiting for the drawbridge to close*
> *then I will proceed to drive home*
> *with caution*

They testified
that I told them
I gave my keys
to a stranger
in the bar
who said he'd drive me home

so after falling asleep
I could only assume
that he stopped the car
on the bridge
and dove off the side
to a watery grave

my lawyer
is calling me to the stand

the courtroom
is one big smile

I think these people like me

PROGRESSIVE SHOTS

For
Bob M.
(when it counted)

BARSTOOL
BACKSLIDE

a
three
piece hoot

at present) what past (would've been

PART ONE

•

PLAN B

fucking world wins again
(didn't think)
lost my job
can't go home
(wife'll flip)
took a left, hit a bar   — (and)

here comes my fifth drink
here comes my fifth drink   — (and)

there is   a god
I call   Vodka   — (and)

a Saint   behind the bar
who   overpours   without pity

me   and   the Saint
had   the joint to   ourselves
since   I showed   up at 2 (p.m.)

until   (half past 5)   as

regurgi-suit/skirt casu-slime
quickly start to densify

so now the Saint's
being buried alive mixing
Liquorice Margaritas

and while pouring back
perhaps   my tenth   —*uhhhmm*
someone   taps me   —*Sir?*

I turn and peer into
the pale of No Excuse who
politely asks me
Have you a Cigaret
I might purchase?

I tell him
Look, kid—No
So don't tap me again
when
the Saint calls out, *Wait!*
grabs a pack off the backbar
and pulls up the flip-top
revealing one left
so
the kid grabs his last smoke
without hesitation
and bypassing Thank You
asks, *You got a match?*

the Saint jerks his thumb
at a bowl on the bar
and he leans close to me
with *Just Watch*

You See
Inside that Cigaret—I put
this Geltab with Chlorine
Which I read when/if inhaled
Will dissolve the Human Lung
And just like this—(snap)—that
Damn conscience-free punk'll be gone

Man—who was I to argue?
The Saint'd been very good to me . . .

now—
me and the Saint watch the once-doomed kid
give the smoke to a girl and light her up

she blows out smoke and sucks in more
then the Saint curses *Shit! Damn thing fell out*

I hold out my hand
thinking
Got no where to be

The Saint hands me the cap

I drop the cap into my drink
and a big, white cloud appears—

perfect time to leave

as the Saint yells to a phone
What do you mean – I dialed 411?

hitting the street, I spot that girl—still
puffing her cig so aimlessly

all that remained was
to find some place
where
the night
belonged to me

PART TWO

·

BROKEN HOME

onward, still mirrored
behind booze
found my stomach
crying out
in a joint
that served food

when I noticed
the fellow
down two stools
eating burger
though garnish
untouched

well

I bid the guy between us
Could you ask that fellow
for his lettuce and tomato——please
if you wouldn't mind?

whereby the guy asked
pointing—but
down two stools
Did mind 'cause
he took his steak knife
and plunged it
impaling
the middle guy's
hand to the bar

then
down two stools
just stood and stared
as middle guy yanked out
the knife from his hand
to sanctify one simple rule
It's not polite to point

and so then
with much further ado
amid mounting threats of *Hey, Chill out, Dude*'s
down two stools chose to belly-flop
across the nearest tabletop
where formerly six patrons sat
with drinks and plates near full

then stood up straight
engaging all
Never talk behind another person's back

then
walked out through
the swinging doors
so I grabbed the ruffage
off his plate and
swallowed—thinking
My Childhood Was Fucked Up, Too

PART THREE

.

MACHINE SWALLOWED

I finally hooked
a redhead at some bar
around midnight—but
(the problem was)
I bought her drink
with my last five
so I tore-ass off to
the nearest ATM
having visions of
every hard cock
on the planet
moving in

I stuck my card
in the machine
pushed the buttons
nothing happened
then
someone put a gun
to my head

I growled
Fucking thing just ate my card
Man, please give me the gun

guy handed me the gun
I shot the machine
twenties popped out
of the slot

I gave back his gun
and (after counting)
half the money
then (pronto)
ran back to
the bar
where the redhead
looked hotter
than even imagined

snapped a crisp twenty
abreast of her breasts—wooing
Order Whatever You Want

my little wife
gently
snoring at home
was
the last thing
on my mind

DOUBLE
(UP/DOWN)

a
two-part
harming
me

.

(prelude)

. .

heard piano
from the street
so, went in and
found a seat, then
a drink was placed
before me, hallowed be

. . .

(A)

.

CONNECTIONS
(NIGHT/DAY)

after floating
through fantasia
the pianoman
settled round
the next stool
smiling, so
I bought us
both a drink
and when
we toasted
to the night
–offhand–
he asked me
You Italian?

so, when
I laughed –nodding
How'd you know?
he answered
Because
Italian's
the only
motherfucker
in this world
ever buy me
a drink

My name's Parnell
I'm 75 years old
—And let me tell you
Man, I got connections

I know
The Ferrini Family
In Boston,
I know
The Luchino Family
In Philly
And—I know
The Abbondonza Family
In Brooklyn

Parnell
paused –slyly
to scope out his blindside
before confessing
In 1980
I killed a motherfucker
and
an hour after
I made my call
the po-lice cut me loose

Why'd you kill the guy?
I asked

Had no choice
he answered
Had to kill
The motherfucker
Man, it was him or me

Parnell
played, we
drank some more;
I think I
sang a song and
somehow remember
searching for my keys
around the bar room floor

when
morning light –split
my head in two
or three or four
while –there before me
sat Parnell
lighting up a cigaret as
some lady shuffled by
slippered pink

undragging smoke
Parnell revealed
That lady you saw's
my wife;
Her name is Noon 'cause
that's when she likes it

then
a small boy
scampered in –screaming
Granpa! Granpa!
There's a white man
dyin' on your sofa

Parnell explained
Don't worry, son
That man
you see's —Italian

I know
The Ferrini Family
In Boston,
I know
The Luchino Family
In Philly
And—I know
The Abbondonza Family
In Brooklyn

(B)
.

AMBLING
(DAY/NIGHT)

while ass-dragging later
through midtown 'bout noon
I swerved past this jerk –with
a nametag on his coat;
you see these fools most everyday
then –sooner wish you hadn't –only
this time I stopped because
my name was stuck to his lapel
and then the guy stopped, too –so
we faced off on the sidewalk
as –to size each other up

his
    tag
    read –Hello
    My Name Is Peter Carlaftes

(I started the ball)
Say—who are you?

(he burst right back)
I'm you!

*Huh?—Whaddaya mean
You're me?*

(he said)
What can I say?
They told me I'm you.

Look! Cut-the-cryptic-crap   —and
tell me who the fuck you are?
And   —who the fuck is "they"?

Okay, pal (he blared)
Here it is
plain and simple
You waste all your time
drinking in the bars,
telling other people
you're a writer of sorts
and since you won't get
with the program
I'm here to pick up the slack
for you pal.

Can't you see?
I'm the productive you!

C'mon now, this is a joke   —I mean
I'm not very big on science fiction
But this sounds more
like some cheap plot

Listen to me
Mister Wish-I-Was-A-Writer
My name is Peter Carlaftes

I introduce innovative software
to quality-minded firms
with a bead on the future

I've got a lovely wife
two beautiful kids,
I didn't run away from
my wife and kids
like you did
you gutless bastard

I own a nice home
and a brand new Lexus

What've you ever done —besides
drink and dream all's well?

(then)
he/me —just
stormed off in a huff
as the people going by
became
blurs

(and) the only thing —that
explained all of this was
it had to be the daylight

well, I made it home
bolted the door —and
for reasons unknown
kept flushing the toilet
over and over —again

until
the night fell —when

I tiptoed down to the local bar
where Joey the Bartender stood
with a giant grin
and a tag (which read)
My Name Is Peter Carlaftes

so I lunged
across the bar   —cursing
Joey, you piece a shit!

while he hosed me down
with the soda gun   —begging
C'mon, let's have a shot

he poured / we drank
he poured —again
Have ten, bejeez
(he muttered)
and when the booze
took hold, I asked   —*Hey*
How'd you set me up?

Well,
me and a pal
you met the guy
we saw you ambling
around midtown

Ambling?
(I leered)

Yeah   —ambling
(he stroked)
Look up the word, Mister Writer

Anyhow,
I told him what to say;
I did it to help wake you up

You see
All the time
you're just sitting here
like you think you got
things all figured out
and if you think
you got things figured out
just where in the hell
do you go from there?

I did it to get you —to
finish something

Here you go
(he poured)

Have another

TWINKLE, TWINKLE

(little bar)

.
one
seam less –time
forever

earlier
　　—shit
didn't look　like
much a night but
when this
hip quartet of chix
started singing
gospel
a cappella
I could only chime in
with some
jazzy counterpart

so now
the cutest one
asks the bartender
Downtown Scott
Who Is That Guy?

not missing a beat
he answers
a drunk
and
Honored,
I'm instantly
full of
myself

myself and
the fleeting
gone

(begins the swirl)

here comes Susan through the door
as boyfriend Tom brings up the rear
who's good for eight ten minutes (tops)
and then one just endures, he waves
an empty stool to my left means
that I'm stuck

I order a double, a beer for Tom and
one more for Bobby (to my right)
then notice Susan hug Andrayla like
the longest lost of friends (although)
last time Susan told me Andrayla
still owes her money for almost a year;
What do I care? It's none of my business
and here comes Tom sipping,
Thanks for the beer

I tell him
My pleasure
(seeing)
Bob, Dave and Donnie
now
over in the corner (are)
setting up to play as soon
as Stevie comes along

and there in the back
the Big Bunny sits
shoving quarters into
the poker machine
right next to Paul
who's trying his unlevel best
to prove to himself that
he's really changed for the better
(whatever the fuck that means)

you see they run the joint
because, I heard last week
after
one long night of drinking
the Bunny and Paul went home
without even counting or hiding the money
(or) let alone locking the gate or the door
so they're on their best behavior until later

(enough said)

Tom
tells me
The snow's
coming down
(so)
I
say
You don't say?
and
he says
Yes
that's right
(entailing)
Reminds
me
of the
Rocky Mountains

apparently,
Bobby liked that cause
he just did a spit take
and burned his nose
with Grand Marnier
(what we call)
Nectar of the Gods

Hey
here comes Bill the Bum

Hey Bill
I ask, *What's shaking?*

he
just stands there
looking nowhere for
what
seems like quite awhile
then unveils
without emotion *look*
I have a proposition

then Tom says *Pete*
I remember this time
hitchhiking through Colorado
once
when me and this guy
that gave me the ride
drove up in the mountains
then sat on the hood and
just laid there and counted stars

You never seen
so many
stars

1
2
3
4 — 5

(Thank God)

Stevie
has arrived
(which means)
Band of George
(their group)
so-called
for another bum
at another bar
(would be)
playing music soon

Tom says
Pete
You gotta hear this
37
38
39

I say
So, Bill
What's on your mind?

he explains the situation

See
I know this woman
that lives in Hell's Kitchen
on West 46th and
the story is this

she'll let you fuck her

Bill points at Bobby
Him, too

I've
been up there
a few times and
I've got her number
but you see, the problem's
I'm too broke to call

I hand Bill a quarter,
point at the phone and
ask him to go make the call

for
some
reason he
stops halfway

Tom
says
Pete
just listen
123
124

I ask Bobby
You coming
with me and Bill?

(Bill just stands there)

now
Bobby and I
work together uptown
for the lowliest life on the planet
and Bobby's been there a lot longer than me
so I ask him
How
can you stand it?
and
he
answers
I
fuck him
to
his
fucking face

nothing
could
be
simpler
than that
(and that is that)

so
I call out
Hey
now
Bill, man
what's the problem?

Tom
says
333
334

Bill
hands me back
the quarter pending
I forgot to tell you that
this woman's got a husband
and I wasn't sure
if that would be a problem

I'm holding out the quarter

Bill
says
He likes to watch

I
say
Hey, Bill
just make the call

Bill takes the quarter back
and
this time gets
as far as the phone
(when)
I hear
Lanie
laugh

the kind of of laugh
you couldn't miss
that is until
you do

Hey
Goodtime
Charlie
How you doing?

he
answers
Breaking
Even

Tom
says
Here's
The best one

909
910

(and)
here comes Bill
with my quarter again

Jesus Bill
What now?

Bill stammers
It's a bit
more involved
than you think

See
I told you
the husband
likes to watch
if he's home

when you're fucking
his wife but
sometimes he gets
a little wound up and
might try to jack off
on your ass
so you gotta promise
you won't punch the guy
or kill him or hurt him
or something like that

Bill, I promise
(gave him the quarter)
and
never saw it
or him again

now the band's about to play
and I see Susan with some guy
she used to fuck
and, right now Tom
ain't finding beauty in the past

wait

the hot chick
with the voice
catches my eye
on her way
out the door
and
even once more
(outside)
through the window

so I tread what
weary led to that
so often magic is
and see her boots
climb through a taxi door
that closed
and purred away
with her and magic
to a distant
never would
(leaving me)

leaning back
on the hood
of
the nearest automobile
to count the many flakes
falling
1
2
3
4
down
(until)

BEEEEEEEEEEEEEEEEEEEEEEEEEEEEEEEEP
this car horn wouldn't stop

I look up at
the clearest sky
and the air is
unmistakably
early summer

(some guy screams)
What's wrong with you?
Yeah—you
I'm
talking
to you
asshole
Get off
the hood of my car

and
where the bar was
once
only
used to be
(now)
and I realize
many years
have
gone
by

bye
bye

and I can't
blame the guy
so I climb off
what's his
(for the moment)
resonating
what is
mine

POETRY

by Peter Carlaftes
Drunk Yard Dog
Drive By Brooding
I Canto Cantos
Nightclub Confidential
Progressive Shots
Sheer Bardom
The Bar Essentials

by Ryan Buynak
Enjoy the Regrets
Yo Quiero Mas Sangre

by Joie Cook
When Night Salutes
the Dawn

by Kathi Georges
Bred for Distance
Punk Rock Journal
Slow Dance at 120 Beats
a Minute

by Karen Hildebrand
One Foot Out the Door
Take a Shot at Love

by Dominique Lowell
Sit Yr Ass Down or You Ain't gettin no
Burger King

by Jane Ormerod
Recreational Vehicles on Fire

by Susan Scutti
We Are Related

by Jackie Sheeler
to[o] long

by The Bass Player from Hand Job
Splitting Hairs

by Angelo Verga
Praise for What Remains

by George Wallace
Poppin' Johnny

PLAYS

by Madeline Artenberg &
Karen Hildebrand
The Old In-and-Out

by Peter Carlaftes
Triumph For Rent (3 Plays)

by Larry Myers
Mary Anderson's Encore
Twitter Theater

HUMOR

by Peter Carlaftes
A Year on Facebook

FICTO-MEMOIR

by Ronnie Norpel
The Constitution Blues

THREE ROOMS PRESS
NEW YORK | threeroomspress.com

CPSIA information can be obtained at www.ICGtesting.com
Printed in the USA
LVOW06s1326071113

359903LV00004B/16/P